Scarface vs. Eliot Ness and the Untouchables: The Lives and Legacies of Al
Capone and Eliot Ness

By Charles River Editors

About Charles River Editors

Charles River Editors was founded by Harvard and MIT alumni to provide superior editing and original writing services, with the expertise to create digital content for publishers across a vast range of subject matter. In addition to providing original digital content for third party publishers, Charles River Editors republishes civilization's greatest literary works, bringing them to a new generation via ebooks.

Visit charlesrivereditors.com for more information.

Introduction

Al Capone (1899-1947)

On February 14, 1929, members of Bugs Moran's North Side gang arrived at a warehouse on North Clark Street in Chicago, only to be approached by several police officers. The officers then marched them outside up against a wall, pulled out submachine guns and shotguns, and gunned them all down on the spot. A famous legend is that one of the shot men, Frank Gusenberg, dying from 14 gunshot wounds, told police that nobody shot him. Though Gusenberg's statement is probably apocryphal, nobody opened their mouths.

Nobody was ever convicted for the "Saint Valentine's Day Massacre," the most famous gangland hit in American history, but it's an open secret that it was the work of America's most famous gangster, Al Capone. Indeed, "Scarface" has captured the nation's popular imagination since Prohibition, managing to be the most notorious gangster in America while living a very visible and high profile life in Chicago.

Born a Brooklyn tough, Capone engaged in a life of crime even as a teenager and had come to Chicago as a young man to smuggle liquor during Prohibition. Allying himself with Johnny Torrio, Capone began to accumulate power almost as quickly as he accumulated a reputation for being merciless, and after an attempted hit severely injured Torrio, the gang's operations were turned over to Capone.

Despite his organized crime spree during the '20s, Capone was a popular figure in Chicago, viewed by many as a Robin Hood because he took pains to make charitable donations to the city. At the same time, he bribed government officials and cops, ensuring they looked the other way despite his violent ways of doing business. Throughout the decade, Capone was often out in public, despite several attempts on his life, and the gang war between Al Capone and Bugs Moran was well known and even celebrated to an extent.

In the end, it wasn't the bodies or the violence that landed Capone in the slammer; it was taxes. After being convicted, Capone managed to continue running his business rackets from behind bars, forcing authorities to move America's most notorious gangster to America's most notorious prison on Alcatraz Island. Capone and Alcatraz only added to each other's lore.

Capone died in 1947, but his life and legacy continue to be the stuff of legends. Even to this day, Chicago's gangster past is viewed as part of the city's lore, and tours of the most famous spots in Chicago's gang history are available across the city. *Scarface vs. Eliot Ness and the Untouchables* looks at the life and crime of Scarface, and the manner in which he has become and remain a staple of American pop culture. Along with pictures of Capone and important people, places, and events in his life, you will learn about America's most infamous gangster like you never have before, in no time at all.

Eliot Ness (1903-1957)

"Unquestionably, it was going to be highly dangerous. Yet I felt it was quite natural to jump at the task. After all, if you don't like action and excitement, you don't go into police work. And, what the hell, I figured, nobody lives forever!" – Eliot Ness

The man most famously associated with Capone's downfall, of course, is Eliot Ness, thanks in large measure to his own sensationalized version of the events that became the basis for the book *Eliot Ness and the Untouchables*." That work in turn spawned the memorable television series "The Untouchables", in which Robert Stack plays an intrepid Eliot Ness who has both seemingly omniscient detective skills and the ability to fight tommy-gun wielding gangsters in street battles.

That portrayal of Ness was a mythological creation made for TV, but it has also cemented his legacy as the man who brought Al Capone down. "The Untouchables" has mostly obscured what the real man and his real work was like during that critical period, but it has also overshadowed the rest of Ness's life and career, which saw him mostly try and fail to parlay his success against Capone into success elsewhere. By the time Ness died, he was mostly down and out, and he had no clue that the book he was working on with writer Oscar Fraley would make him one of the most famous law enforcement officials in American history. Some have even dubbed him the patron saint of today's ATF.

Scarface vs. Eliot Ness and the Untouchables looks at the life and career of Eliot Ness, but it also humanizes the man who refused Capone's bribes and never flinched. Along with pictures of important people, places, and events, you will learn about Eliot Ness like you never have before, in no time at all.

Chapter 1: The State of America in the Early 20ᵗʰ Century

The early decades of the 20ᵗʰ century featured a series of growing pains for the United States as the nation entered a new century, a rapidly changing world, and a new stage in its own evolution. All at once, it seemed, American society was attempting to deal with the excesses and injustices of a rapidly industrializing and increasingly centralized economy, a wave of immigration changing the ethnic make-up of the country, and the emergence of new social movements fighting for causes like women's right to vote.

A driving political force during these years was the Progressive Movement, which on the one hand sought to ensure consumer and worker rights, and offset the growing power of big business. On the other hand, many backers of Progressivism were staunch capitalists intent on "rationalizing" capitalism to protect it from a possible threat posed by socialism, which, while much stronger in Europe, enjoyed considerable support in early 20ᵗʰ century America. Finally, Progressives echoed some of the moral concerns raised in the Third Great Awakening, a religious revival that swept America during the latter stages of the 1800s. Though the Progressive Movement began to dissipate during World War I, the Prohibition Act passed in 1919 and implemented in 1920 can be seen as Progressivism's last gasp.

It was on this contradictory stage—a nation with one foot in the 19ᵗʰ century and another in the 20ᵗʰ—that Al Capone famously and infamously strutted his stuff. He was the face of a multi-ethnic urban America, an early innovator in an almost corporate approach to organized crime, and a savvy manipulator of big-city politics. His mixture of sophistication and savagery mirrored that of a nation trying to harness its considerable but sometimes unruly energies. It was America's brief and disastrous attempt to outlaw the sale of alcohol—an experiment that in so many ways seemed at odds with a decade some have called The Roaring Twenties—that allowed Capone to garner the tremendous wealth and wield the outrageous power that made him an almost mythical, larger-than-life historical figure. And it was another of Progressivism's reforms, the establishment of a Federal Income Tax, which would in the end provide for Capone's downfall.

The Era of Progressive Reform

In the final decades of the 1800s, the United States was reshaped by the second wave of its Industrial Revolution, a fundamental economic transformation that included the building of transcontinental railroads, the explosive rise of the iron and steel industries, the birth of the automobile industry, and the widespread implementation of modernized factory production. These changes produced great wealth and an improved quality of life for many, but considerable social upheaval as well. Traditional jobs on farms and in small trades were replaced by jobs in sweltering and often dangerous factories. Companies seeking competitive edge exploited underage and immigrant labor. The rapid growth of cities outpaced their ability to take care of the poor and disadvantaged.

In the early 1900s, a new generation of crusading journalists known as "muckrakers" campaigned to expose the social ills and abuses of power produced by unchecked capitalism. Their exposes resulted in reforms including child labor laws, the creation of the Food and Drug Administration, and the breaking up of the Standard Oil Company. Progressivism was less a movement than a set of ideals embraced by politicians from both major parties. Teddy Roosevelt, who took over the Presidency in 1901 after William McKinley's assassination and was reelected in a landslide in 1904, was one of the most prominent faces of Progressivism. He pushed for active enforcement of antitrust laws (proudly declaring himself a "trust-buster") and overall greater regulation of industry, and was an early voice for conservationism.

Progressives took up a variety of other causes, including civil service reforms to combat the power of big-city "machine" politics, as well as compulsory education laws. Though forward-looking in many ways, Progressivism was also nostalgic for the clearer morality of a bygone agrarian era, naively believing that government and industry could be made squeaky clean through the application of "scientific" principles. The support many Progressives lent to Prohibition reflects that naiveté.

Labor Strife and the "Red Scare"

With the exception of the IWW (International Workers of the World), organized labor was strongly supportive of the war effort, minimizing strikes and encouraging members to enlist. Union membership swelled during the war, and union leaders were hopeful that their wartime patriotism would be rewarded afterward. But a rocky and uneven economy led to an unprecedented number of strikes in 1919, as many as 3600 in total. Wartime unity was quickly forgotten as the government brought in troops to help quell a shipyard workers' strike in Seattle, a police strike in Boston, and later a series of strikes by steelworkers that resulted in the deaths of dozens of workers. Unions were charged with being "sovietism in disguise," and even President Wilson denounced the striking Boston police as "Bolsheviks."

The so-called "Red Scare" had its roots in wartime propaganda, and the government's insistence on "100% Americanism." But in the midst of the economic uncertainty and labor unrest that followed the war, "anti-Bolshevik" agitation only intensified. A series of unsuccessful bombings in early 1919 prompted Attorney General Palmer to create a new anti-radical division within the Justice Department's Bureau of Investigation (which in 1924 became the FBI). The head of the new division, J. Edgar Hoover, thus began a decades-long crusade against so-called "subversives." The Red Scare peaked later that year and early the next. In November 1919, Emma Goldman and 248 other radicals were deported and sent on a ship to the Soviet Union, and in a series of raids in January, as many as 6000 were arrested. But Palmer's warnings of a massive May Day uprising failed to materialize; and abroad, Bolshevism was contained in the

Soviet Union and failed, as many had feared, to spread to Europe. Weary of conflict and politics, the American people embraced new President Warren Harding's "return to normalcy" and the Red Scare fizzled as quickly as it had flared up.

World War I and Its Aftermath

When war broke out in Europe in 1914, the United States was determined to maintain a neutral stance. Woodrow Wilson won the 1916 election on a platform of keeping the nation out of war. But German submarine attacks on British ships like the Lusitania (which resulted in hundreds of American deaths) finally prompted Congress to declare war on Germany in 1917. About 1.4 million men saw actual combat—53,000 of whom were killed, and over 200,000 injured. These numbers were high considering America's brief involvement in the war: the first U.S. troops arrived in June 1917, but didn't see significant action until the following spring. Within six months, the war was over. However, Allied troops remained in the area through 1920. The focus of their continued involvement was fear of the new Communist government in Russia (now the Soviet Union) that had overthrown the Czar in 1917, forcing Russia out of the war.

The war brought about a wide range of changes on the home front. President Wilson created a Committee on Public Information to generate wartime propaganda and instill patriotism. In its zeal to create unity at home, the government encouraged a backlash against immigrants, Germans especially, and branded all opposition to the war as "Bolshevism." Women were drafted into the wartime effort at home, and their participation created a heightened expectation for equal rights that helped lead to the 19th Amendment. The war also had a significant impact on black Americans. The closing off of immigration produced sudden labor shortages in Northern factories, prompting the initial stages of what is known as the Great Migration of black Americans from the South to the North. Also, the 400,000 black men who served in the military returned home with new hopes of a more equal footing in society. Finally, the extensive involvement of the government in the economy during the war, which included taking over the railroads, set the stage for a backlash against governmental intervention in the postwar years.

Chapter 2: Capone's Early Years

Young Al Capone with his mother

Roots in Naples

Although Al Capone will forever be associated with Chicago, he was a native Brooklyn tough with an unmistakable Italian background. Capone was not—as he often insisted, and as early accounts of his life claimed—born in Italy. His parents, Gabriele and Teresa, along with their first two children, arrived in New York in 1894, five years before Capone was born. They had come from Naples, a seaside city in the south of Italy, and the country's third largest. Naples was known for its long history of political instability, having fallen under the rule of a number of foreign powers, and also playing a role in the country's ongoing internal strife. Its government was weak, and into the political void stepped an organized crime syndicate called the Camorra, which infiltrated city government so thoroughly, especially the police department, that local officials sometimes turned to them to ensure public safety.

Chicago, the American city where Capone eventually ended up, was in many ways the American equivalent to Naples: a working-class, unruly and divided city that was a perfect breeding ground for organized crime. The parallels between how the Camorra operated in Naples and how Capone operated in Chicago are fascinating and undeniable, and it would be Capone who masterfully exploited them.[1]

Prejudice against Italian-Americans

The initial wave of Italian immigration in the late 1800s consisted mainly of single men

---

[1] Bergreen, *Capone*, p. 26

seeking to make some money and then return home to Italy, but Capone's parents were part of a new breed intent on staying and making a new life in the United States. There they indeed found opportunity, but also found themselves at the bottom of the ethnic pecking order. Italians were looked down on by most as the least desirable and least capable of the new immigrants. Even Jacob Riis, a crusading journalist and social reformer who exposed the appalling conditions of immigrants in his famous book *How the Other Half Lives,* concurred with this assessment: "The Italian comes in at the bottom… and stays there."[2]

Making matters even worse, among Italian immigrants, those from Southern Italy were viewed as the lowest of the low. Indeed, even back in Italy, Southern Italians had been the object of the scorn of their Northern countrymen. At the same time, this shared prejudice didn't exactly bring Capone and other Italian-Americans with roots in Naples closer to their Sicilian compatriots. Throughout his life, Capone would distance himself from, and find himself at odds with, Sicilian organized crime leaders.

Capone's Childhood

Capone's early years in New York were certainly not easy ones, but his childhood was hardly one of destitution. His father was a barber who eventually came to own his own shop, and the family moved around in Brooklyn through a series of progressively nicer apartments. Neighbors later remembered the family as quiet and respectable. Capone for his part was a solid B-student through the fifth grade, and though he was involved in the occasional neighborhood scuffle, he was not an especially troublesome child.

The following year, however, young Alphonse reached a turning point. Al started missing school and was asked to repeat the 6th grade. When a teacher reprimanded him for misconduct and struck him (not unusual at the time), the boy struck back and was expelled. Still in his early teens, young Al Capone never returned to school. Yet even this early rebellion was not remarkable, and it didn't inevitably mark the young Capone for a life of crime. In fact, it was unusual for immigrant children to move on to high school anyway.

It was where Al decided to start hanging out that set him down his notorious path. Young Al began spending a good part of his days at a local pool hall and became quite proficient at the game. Just down the street was the headquarters of Johnny Torrio, a local racketeer who would later take Capone under his wings and become Scarface's most important mentor. Al started out running small errands for Torrio, and it was in these early stages that he proved himself to be reliable and trustworthy.

---

[2] quoted in Bergreen, *Capone,* p. 22

Giovanni "Johnny" Torrio

As he grew older, Capone occasionally flirted with local gang activity, but otherwise appeared headed on a respectable if unremarkable path. He worked for three years at a munitions factory, and later as a paper cutter. The adolescent Capone enjoyed dressing up and going out, but didn't especially stand out from others. The novelist Daniel Fuchs remembered him as "something of a nonentity, affable, soft of speech and even mediocre in everything but dancing."[3]

Though Capone's time at clubs like the Broadway Casino was innocent enough, he also began hanging out at the Adonis Social Club, which attracted a more volatile crowd. It was in the Adonis basement, where guests were known to engage in target practice shooting at beer bottles, that Al learned how to handle a revolver and likely developed a taste for the kind of crowd he would later run with.

Capone Contracts Syphilis

It wasn't unusual for young men like Capone to find their first sexual encounters among the local prostitutes, and it is almost certain that it was around this time that Al contracted syphilis. Awareness of venereal disease was only just beginning to take hold among public health officials, triggered in part by screenings during the war-time draft in which 10% of the young men tested positive.

Syphilis (whose origins can be traced, ironically, to Naples) has three distinct stages. The first two are relatively benign and consist of genital sores and then flu-like symptoms, both of which usually go away on their own. Among an unlucky 20%, the disease then goes into an extended latent phase, its later third stage subtle but deadly, and often undiagnosed because its victims have long assumed the disease went away on its own. The third stage attacks the frontal lobe of

---

[3] Bergreen, *Capone*, p. 43

the brain in somewhat the same ways as Alzheimer's, but gradually and over many years. It eventually results in dementia, but long before that produces a series of personality changes and distortions that include irritability, sudden mood swings, and megalomania. Though Capone's symptoms didn't become glaring until much later, recent biographers credit the disease with playing a central role in Al's transformation from an unremarkable youth only occasionally caught up in trouble to a volatile and feared ringleader of organized crime. The disease would also be blamed for Capone's later descent into dementia near the end of his life.

"Scarface"

It was under the influence of local racketeer Johnny Torrio that young Al Capone began veering from any semblance of a life of respectability. One of Torrio's associates, the gangster and hitman Frankie Yale, had just opened a bar on Coney Island he called the Harvard Club (though it was hardly an Ivy League-type establishment). He needed someone who could double as a bartender and bouncer, and Torrio recommended the 17 year old Capone. Yale and Capone hit it off, and Al became a fixture at the new club.

Frankie Yale

A year into his tenure, Al was waiting a table and in a lapse of judgment made a suggestive remark about a young lady seated there. Her brother, drunk and outraged, leapt up in her defense and in the scuffle that followed ended up slashing Capone several times across the face with a knife. Though there was a good deal of blood, the damage was not serious, but the scars remained visible for the rest of Capone's life, and he was greatly self-conscious and vain about them. He concocted cover stories that included one about the scars being a war injury, even though he never served. He even went so far as to cover them up with make-up, and insisted on being photographed on the side where the scars didn't show. He hated his unofficial (and still best known) nickname "Scarface," preferring "Snorky," slang at the time for someone who was a stylish dresser.

Capone's very visible scars on his left cheek

Despite that incident, Capone's standing with Frankie Yale was such that he was allowed to stay on at the Harvard Club, and Capone even subsequently used his attacker, Frank Gallucio, as a bodyguard. Moreover, his duties were expanded to include helping his boss collect on unpaid debts, a task that in 1919 led to a far more serious of act of violence when Al ended up shooting a man who wouldn't pay up on a gambling debt. This, too, ended up becoming part of the Capone legend: that he shortly after fled to Chicago to escape a murder rap. But in fact Al's path to Chicago and a full-time life of organized crime was not so direct.

Marriage and Family

Around this same time, Al began looking for more lasting romantic companionship. He became smitten with a free-spirited Italian girl just down the street, but apparently her parents didn't find Capone to be a suitable match, so he began searching elsewhere. At a club further away where the Italian neighborhood bordered the Irish, he met a quiet Irish girl named Mary Coughlin. At first glance, this seemed like an odd match, since she was not Italian and came from a solid middle-class family. But despite these very obvious differences, she was instantly smitten with Al, and she would remain devoted to him the rest of their life together in spite of his criminal activities and frequent womanizing.

Mae Capone

It wasn't long before Mae, as she was known, became pregnant, giving birth to their first child, Sonny, in early December of 1918. As a young child, Sonny suffered from frequent infections and loss of hearing, likely a result of Capone's syphilis. It wasn't until later that month that the couple actually married, a wedding that occurred at least in part so Al could avoid the draft.

Now a family man, Capone once more set himself on a path of respectability, not only leaving Frankie Yale and the Harvard Club, but deciding his youthful stomping grounds might not make the best place to raise a family. In early 1920 he relocated to Baltimore and found work as a bookkeeper for a construction company, where he displayed solid accounting skills and a good head for numbers. But no sooner had he established his new life when his father suddenly passed away later that year. Al's oldest brother had shipped out west, and the next youngest, Ralph, was in no position to take responsibility for the widowed Teresa and the three younger children.

While back in town for the funeral, Al resumed contact with Johnny Torrio, who around this time had decided that Prohibition-era Chicago was where the real money could be made, and he had already begun working for the city's top organized crime figure. Torrio persuaded his young protégé to follow him, and in early 1921 Capone gave his notice to the construction firm and headed west.[4]

Chapter 3: Ness's Early Years

Eliot Ness was born in Chicago on April 19, 1903, the youngest of five children born to Peter and Emma Ness. Eliot was a later life child 13 years younger than his nearest sibling, and by the time he came along, his Norwegian immigrant parents had built a successful middle class life through hard work and clean living. Well into middle age by the time he was born, Eliot's parents lavished their youngest with plenty of attention and maintained high expectations for him.

Through the years Peter was able to build up his small wholesale bakery, and the well-behaved Eliot often helped his father in the bakery in order to earn spending money. He also had a paper route and was an excellent student at Christian Fenger High School. When not working or studying, he spent his free time reading adventure stories, especially the tales of Sherlock Holmes. His brother-in-law, Alexander Jamie, happened to be an agent with the Justice Department, and in addition to encouraging Eliot's interest in mysteries and law enforcement, he also taught Eliot to shoot.

After graduating from high school, Ness enrolled in the University of Chicago, where he earned a degree in economics. While there he also joined the Sigma Alpha Epsilon fraternity, played tennis and practiced jujitsu. Then, in 1925, he disappointed his parents for the first time in his life when he went to work as an investigator for the Retail Credit Company. Even worse, he continued his education with night classes, not toward an MBA, but for a Master's Degree in Criminal Justice.

In 1927, Ness received his degree in criminology and took a job with the Treasury Department. With Jamie's help, Ness won a transfer to the Prohibition Bureau. Ness would end up making a name for himself there by being one of the few agents unwilling to take a bribe or look the other way when organized criminals threatened him.

Though Prohibition was ultimately a poorly conceived and poorly implemented disaster, it is not as simple a story as it might first appear to be. The Temperance Movement, as it was first known, dated all the way back to the 1840s, when drinking was an undeniable problem in American life. Historians estimate that per capita consumption of booze was as high as 7 gallons of pure alcohol a year, well over three times the current rate, and the equivalent of 90 bottles of 80-proof liquor a year. In response to this very real problem, groups like the Daughters of Temperance began cropping up, and later the Women's Christian Temperance Union. The

---

[4] Bergreen, p. 58

Prohibition Party was founded in 1872, but it was the Anti-Saloon League, founded in 1893, that made prohibition a viable political force.

Temperance was connected in unexpected ways to a variety of other causes. The WCTU was at the center of the women's suffrage movement: it provided a training ground for women in political activism, and women concerned about moral issues like drinking realized they would have greater impact if given the right to vote. Most prominent abolitionists were in favor of temperance, as were prominent black leaders like Frederick Douglass and Booker T. Washington. Prohibition also attracted activists of a very different sort: beer and saloons were very much associated with the new wave of immigration, and the ASL in particular had a strongly anti-immigrant bent. Thus, the politics of the temperance movement was all over the map, and made for strange and contradictory alliances.

Prohibition also came to be connected with the campaign for a federal income tax. The alcohol excise tax accounted for a substantial amount of the government's budget, forcing supporters of Prohibition to answer the question of how to replace that income, and thus creating additional momentum for the 16th Amendment approved in 1913. And conversely, the need to bolster the federal budget in the early days of the Depression became one of many reasons cited for Prohibition's repeal.

Passing Prohibition was one thing, but enforcing it was another, and in many ways Prohibition seemed doomed from the start. The new Prohibition Bureau was a part of the Treasury Department, whose head, Andrew Mellon, never fully supported the law. The Bureau was given only 1500 field agents to start with, and much of the hiring of agents was influenced by the Anti-Saloon League, which used the positions to pay back political favors from the Prohibition campaign. In a fascinating historical footnote, it turns out Capone's eldest brother, who had earlier moved out West and disappeared from sight, reinvented himself under a new name and became a well-known and highly regarded Prohibition Agent. He eventually reconnected with his family, visiting them yearly in Chicago and largely managing to keep his two lives separate.

The ways of circumventing Prohibition were many and varied. Whiskey and gin and rum were smuggled in through Canada and the Bahamas, among other places. A line of ships along the East Coast permanently docked just beyond the three-mile border, and essentially serving as liquor warehouses, was known as Rum Row. Doctors were allowed to write prescriptions for "medicinal" alcohol, and exemptions for wine designated for Communion were available. In addition to all the money to be made from outright bootlegging, apparently legitimate businesses thrived as well: for example, the number of Walgreens pharmacies shot up from 20 to 525 over the course of the 1920s. Foreign travel shot up, and ship lines developed "cruises to nowhere" or "booze cruises."

Disenchantment with Prohibition grew steadily as the decade progressed. So-called "dry" crusaders didn't help their cause with overly zealous measures like the Jones Law, which aimed to make all violations of Prohibition a felony. But it was the stock market crash and the Depression that was the nail in the coffin for Prohibition. Voters were disillusioned with the Republican Party, and in the 1932 election FDR argued that the government desperately needed the income from alcohol taxes. To a large extent that was accurate; during the first year of Repeal, such taxes accounted for 9% of all federal revenue. In February 1933, the 21st Amendment (repealing the 18th) was introduced, and when in December the necessary number of states had ratified it, Prohibition's 14 year history was over.

Among Prohibition's long-term (and unintended) consequences was the nationalization of organized crime. The complex transportation schemes required to move liquor like Canadian whiskey across the border, then to New York, and then on to Chicago also fostered the creation of regional and national networks among racketeers and bootleggers. Organized crime became organized and bureaucratized as never before. As historian Selwyn Raab wrote in *The Five Families,* "Prohibition had been the catalyst for transforming the neighborhood gangs of the 1920s into smoothly run regional and national criminal corporations... Bootlegging gave them on-the-job executive training."[5]

Chapter 4: Capone's Rise to Power

Chicago in 1920

Founded in 1832, and through the mid-1800s a largely provincial regional hub, Chicago was rebuilt after the Great Fire of 1871 as a modern city made of steel and iron and granite. By 1920 its population was nearly 3 million, the second largest in the country, and it was the undisputed capital of mid-America. Dominated economically by industries like meatpacking, lumber and the railroads, Chicago was a richly diverse and heavily segregated city.

Lacking the established elite and long-standing cultural traditions of eastern cities like New York and Boston, Chicago was notable for its loose and open nature. It was a city in which an ambitious businessman (or gangster) could make an almost immediate impact. In the eyes of many, its looseness extended to matters of morality as well. In his 1904 book *The Shame of the Cities,* muckraking journalist Lincoln Steffens summed the city up this way: "First in violence, deepest in dirt; loud, lawless, unlovely, ill-smelling, irreverent... the 'tough' among cities, a spectacle for the nation."[6]

---

[5] quoted in Okrent, *Last Call,* p. 345
[6] Bergreen, p. 77

Torrio Consolidates Power

Johnny Torrio was summoned to Chicago to be the right-hand man for James "Big Jim" Colosimo, who had emerged from the post-war years as the leader of the city's most prominent organized crime syndicate. Colosimo lived large and extravagantly, and he saw the business-like and unassuming Torrio as a perfect match. The cornerstone of Colosimo's expanding empire was a large network of brothels, and the new Prohibition laws provided yet another possibility for growth. Even before this expansion, Colosimo came into frequent conflict with the Black Hand, which had prompted his association with Torrio in the first place. When Torrio first introduced Capone to Chicago, Capone worked as a bouncer and bartender at one of Colosimo's brothels, the Four Deuces.

However, Torrio's arrival on the scene happened to coincide with Colosimo's rapid and unexpected demise. Big Jim fell fast and hard for a young actress and singer, and rashly divorced his wife and former business partner, leaving the day-to-day operations almost entirely to Torrio. Because of this, as well as his reluctance to engage in liquor smuggling, Colosimo was increasingly perceived as vulnerable, a situation that was quickly taken advantage of by Torrio. When Big Jim returned to Chicago after his recent second marriage, Torrio called him to let him know that a shipment was arriving at his café. When Colosimo showed up at the café to get the package, he was shot and killed.

Though nobody was ever convicted, it has long been assumed that Colosimo's assassin was none other than Frankie Yale, Torrio's and Capone's old associate back in New York. By this time Yale had established himself as one of the most prominent gangsters in New York City, but perhaps jealous of Torrio's new success in Chicago and wishing to make his own mark, Yale travelled to Chicago and on May 11, 1920 he allegedly took out Colosimo in the first of many notorious gangland hits to come. Yale was picked up after an eyewitness identified him, but he was later released when the witness claimed his memory had failed him. Capone himself also continues to be a suspected assassin of Big Jim.

Big Jim Colosimo

Big Jim may have been going soft, but he had done a credible job of organizing a criminal syndicate, and regardless of who murdered Big Jim, the political climate in Chicago was a perfect setting for Torrio to establish himself in the wake of Colosimo's killing. New mayor "Big Bill" Thompson openly promised to turn a blind eye to the Prohibition laws—declaring that Chicago was "wet," and so was he. Torrio quickly ingratiated himself with the Thompson administration and began expanding the network he inherited from Colosimo, as well as establishing peace with a number of the many other crime syndicates in the city. It wasn't long before his operation included thousands of speakeasies, brothels, and gambling joints. Torrio needed some men he could trust to help him run his new empire, and it was at that point that he turned to his 22 year old protégé Al Capone.

Mayor "Big Bill" Thompson

Capone Settles In

Capone initially moved out on his own, followed shortly by older brother Ralph, and the two started out managing a handful of brothels for Torrio. Capone's other older brother, Frank, also moved out and joined the Torrio operation. Less than a year later, Al was named manager of the Four Deuces, a saloon and gambling den that served as the headquarters of Torrio's empire. It was a significant promotion, and Al was now put on a salary. Showing his growing business savvy, Capone set up a couple of front businesses—one identifying him as a second-hand furniture dealer, as well as a second office opened under the alias "A. Brown, MD" complete with a waiting room with bottles of legal medicinal alcohol on display.

Ralph "Bottles" Capone

With his wife and son still back in Brooklyn, Al lived the high life and started to get carried away. Driving drunk one night, he crashed into a parked taxi and, irrationally enraged at the cabbie, pulled a gun on him and flashed a fake sheriff's badge. The incident resulted in the first of Capone's arrests, followed just as quickly by his quiet release after Torrio pulled the necessary strings. Later that year, in 1922, Al had enough money to buy a nice home on a quiet street, and he soon sent for his wife and son, as well as his widowed mother, younger brothers, and sister. Capone reestablished a lower profile, and for several years no one in the neighborhood suspected he was anything but a respectable businessman.

Expanding to the Suburbs

After eight scandal-ridden years in office, the permissive "Big Bill" Thompson was finally forced to withdraw from the 1923 mayoral election, and his successor, William Dever, vowed to make a radical change in direction—not only enforcing Prohibition, but cracking down on organized crime. The new policy heightened tension between the various gangs competing for a share of all the illegal profits to be had in Chicago, and it brought about the early stages of a long series of turf wars in the city.

Mayor William Dever

Torrio's response was to keep a low profile in Chicago itself and shift the focus of operations to the suburbs. Thus, Torrio and Capone chose Cicero, a sleepy working-class suburb whose residents loved their beer but were more conservative when it came to vices like prostitution. In late 1923, Torrio set up the first two of many brothels to come, established a profit-sharing arrangement with rival gangs, and then left Capone in charge while he took some time off to move his aging mother back to Italy. In an effort spearheaded by older brother Frank—who with his tall good looks was the most publicly visible of the Capone brothers—the Capones began a systematic effort to take control of Cicero's political establishment. They put up their own candidates, intimidated the opposition, and stole ballot boxes, whatever it took: and sure enough, the Capone-backed candidates were swept into office by wide margins.

With Cicero's City Hall in his back pocket, Capone and his brothers engaged in aggressive expansion, establishing a large new brothel in the neighboring suburb of Forest View (which came to be called "Caponeville"), a major new gambling hall, and taking over the local racetrack. The only opposition the brothers encountered came from the local paper, the *Cicero Tribune,* run by a high-minded journalist named Robert St. John.

Capone Loses a Brother

As the political primaries of 1924 approached, the stream of critical coverage from St. John finally had an effect. The far more influential *Chicago Tribune* picked up the story, predicting intimidation and violence in the upcoming elections, and a crusading judge convinced Mayor Dever to let him deputize members of the Chicago police force, who otherwise had no jurisdiction in Cicero, to monitor the elections and ensure peace. The plan backfired as the fleet of 70 cops arrived in plain clothes and in unmarked black sedans similar to those used by the Capones and other gangs. When Frank Capone saw a long line of black cars arrive and the non-uniformed police began to get out, he assumed they represented a rival gang, reached for his gun and was mowed down by the police, who fired dozens of shots. Though the police would later claim Frank fired at the officers first, other bystanders claimed Frank did nothing more than reach for his gun. On April 4, 1924, Frank was given a quintessential mob funeral, replete with $20,000 worth of flowers (ironically bought from one of Capone's gangster rivals, Dion O'Banion) and a huge motorcade.

A grief-stricken Al was now more determined than ever to ruthlessly acquire and exercise power. Only Torrio, back from Italy, convinced him not to declare war on the Chicago police. Nevertheless, Capone's rage spilled over five weeks after the funeral when his good friend Jack Guzik was insulted by a small-time hoodlum, for which Capone sought out and killed the man. As would happen again and again, several eyewitnesses to the shooting suddenly developed a case of poor memory, and despite a state attorney's best efforts to indict Capone, no charges were ever filed.

Chapter 5: Gang Violence Erupts

The "Beer Wars"

Although Torrio tried to maintain the peace among Chicago's many racketeers and organized crime syndicates, turf battles in what the press called the "Beer Wars" began breaking out and escalating. So-called "gangland-style" murders rose from 29 in 1922 to 52 in 1923. One of the major players in the war—the Irish gangster Dion O'Banion, the most prominent organized crime figure on the North Side—made a small fortune through the flower shop he ran as his front business: it became accepted practice, even for rival gangs, to order flowers for the constant stream of gang funerals through his shop.

O'Banion

The other major players in the Beer Wars were the six Genna brothers, a tough and volatile group of Sicilian bootleggers. Torrio and Capone maintained an uneasy peace with them, but tension ran high between the Gennas and O'Banion and ultimately full-scale war broke out. O'Banion hijacked one of the Gennas' trucks, and then in an ambitious double-crossing scheme leaked a tip to the police that set up Torrio and Capone to be arrested at a brewery the three of them jointly owned. Capone escaped, but Torrio did not. Though he was soon out on bail, even Torrio gave up on keeping the peace, and in November of 1924 he and Capone teamed up with the Genna brothers and arranged a dramatic slaying of O'Banion in his own flower shop. For the hit, Torrio and Capone relied on an old acquaintance: none other than Frankie Yale. When Yale entered O'Banion's flower shop with gunmen John Scalise and Albert Anselmi, O'Banion recognized him and greeted him with a handshake. Yale then held onto O'Banion's hand while Scalise and Anselmi fired bullets into O'Banion's chest, cheeks, and throat, killing him on the spot.

The murder of O'Banion only heightened the now burgeoning gang war between the hoods on the North Side and the Torrio/Capone syndicate on the South Side. The violence continued unabated as O'Banion's allies—including "Hymie" Weiss and "Bugs" Moran—fought to hold onto O'Banion's North Side turf and exact revenge for his murder. Still facing charges and an inevitable trial, Torrio exited the scene for Hot Springs, Arkansas, again leaving Capone in charge. Knowing he was a target, Al took heightened security measures, but even still he just narrowly escaped an assassination attempt by Weiss, Moran, and Vincent "The Schemer" Drucci on January 25, 1925, who riddled Capone's car. The failed attack featured a new weapon on the Chicago gang scene: the Thompson submachine gun, or "tommy gun" as it would popularly be known. Capone quickly acquired his own arsenal, and the Beer Wars took on a new savagery.

Hymie Weiss

Bugs Moran

Two days later, Torrio was himself the object of an assassination attempt. As Torrio was heading toward his apartment after shopping with his wife, Weiss, Moran and Vincent Drucci poured gunfire into Torrio's car, hitting him in the jaw, lungs, groin, legs, and abdomen. Moran walked up to finish Torrio off with a shot to the head but had run out of ammunition, and the three assailants fled before making sure Torrio was dead. Somehow, the severely wounded Torrio managed to survive, spending weeks recovering in the hospital, with Capone providing protection around the clock. He healed only to have to finally face the federal charges that came out of the brewery raid. Though convicted and sentenced to serve nine months, the wounded Torrio pulled the necessary strings and had an easy time of it in jail in a well-furnished private cell. Upon being released, he announced his retirement and was spirited away to New York. Happy to make it out alive, Torrio told Capone, "It's all yours Al. Me? I'm quitting. It's Europe for me."

Capone was now fully in charge of the Chicago Outfit

Vincent "The Schemer" Drucci

Capone the Public Figure

Despite his rapid rise to power, Al Capone had until now largely stayed out of the public eye. A number of media stories following Frank's murder failed, in fact, to even get his name right. But upon assuming control of Torrio's organization in the spring of 1925, Capone relocated the center of his operations to a high-profile hotel, the Metropole, and made a new effort to enter and remain in the limelight. He carefully fashioned a public image, not as a gangster, but as a well-dressed, charismatic businessman. He became close friends with the journalist Harry Read, who helped school Capone on his public image, and Capone began appearing at public events like baseball games. He even made almost daily visits to City Hall, and though he had no interest in public office, he carried himself like an elected official.

Capone undeniably struck an impressive public figure. Already very wealthy, Capone traveled in style, frequently wearing custom suits, chomping on cigars, enjoying good food and drink, and frequently accompanied by women. Clearly a celebrity, he and the media relished each other, and it was through the media that Capone delivered the classic quotes he was known for: "I am just a businessman, giving the people what they want," and "All I do is satisfy a public demand."

Of course, nobody was more aware than Capone what kind of danger he was actually in. Hand-in-hand with his new public visibility, Capone implemented a series of extravagant security measures. His new headquarters at the Metropole included a network of tunnels originally built for hauling coal but now refurbished as alternate exits. He traveled in a customized armored Cadillac sedan that weighed seven tons and was always accompanied by a convoy of bodyguards. "Hymie" Weiss and "Bugs" Moran were still bitter over O'Banion's murder and had one by one picked off several of the Genna brothers. Capone figured sooner or later they would come after him again.

Massacre in New York

In late 1925, Al Capone took a trip back east with a highly personal agenda, but also a business one. The personal agenda concerned an emergency operation for his son Sonny, who continued to suffer from a variety of health problems. Back east, Capone sought the best treatment money could buy, and got it. With Sonny's operation a success, Capone took care of some business in New York, meeting with his old associate Frankie Yale to establish a pipeline for bootlegging Canadian whiskey through New York and then on to Chicago. Their business complete, Frankie offered to host a Christmas night celebration at one of his old haunts, the Adonis Social Club, with Al as his honored guest.

Brooklyn at that time was in the midst of its own gang war, with Yale and the Italians against Richard Lonergan and the Irish. Yale received a tip the night before that Lonergan was going to target the party, and his first instinct was to cancel the celebration. But Capone glimpsed an opportunity and arranged an ambush. A fierce gun battle took place inside the club, killing Lonergan and three of his associates. In one bloody Christmas night, Capone had strengthened his alliance with Yale, put his fellow Italians in charge of Brooklyn, and established Chicago as the new center of power in organized crime.

But is that how it actually went down? Some have claimed that this is another embellished tale in the legend of Al Capone. According to author Patrick Downey, the killing of Lonergan and his associates at the Adonis Club was not an ambush but more likely an unplanned, spur of the moment shooting that came about in response to a drunken argument between Capone and Lonergan's associate, Needles Ferry. Witnesses also reported Lonergan and his crew were heavily intoxicated and shouting ethnic slurs at bar patrons. However, according to reports, when police found Ferry and Lonergan, they'd been shot execution style.

A Public Official Is Murdered

Chicago had seen its share of notorious murders over the course of the 1920s, but the killing of an assistant state attorney in the spring of 1926 truly shocked a city that wasn't easily shocked, and it triggered a crisis that would ultimately discredit city and state officials alike.

In a bizarre night that would take months for authorities to unravel, William McSwiggin, the attorney who had tried to indict Capone for murder back in 1924, got caught up in a Cicero turf war between Capone and two rival bootleggers, the O'Donnell brothers. While maintaining a tough-on-crime public image, privately McSwiggin had made accommodations with a number of gangsters, including Capone. With a penchant for vice as a card player, gambler, and drinker, McSwiggin naturally came into contact with and even befriended Al Capone.

On this night in 1926, however, McSwiggin chanced into meeting up with the O'Donnells after he had been out drinking and his car broke down. That same night, the brothers made a fateful decision to go cruising in Cicero, and the group made their way to the Pony Inn, a Capone-run speakeasy near Capone's headquarters in Cicero. Capone got word that the O'Donnells' Lincoln had been spotted cruising his territory, interpreted this as a provocation, and had the group (which also included the sons of two cops) gunned down as they exited a local bar.

As fate would have it, the O'Donnells escaped, but McSwiggin and the two young men were killed. While Capone went into hiding, the city was in an uproar over the killing of a well-known prosecutor whose seedy connections were a mystery known only amongst his associates. The newspapers were full of speculation, and McSwiggin's boss, state attorney Robert Crowe, publicly declared his belief that Capone was behind the murder. He deputized 300 detectives who scoured Cicero and Chicago, looking for clues. Over the course of six months, six separate grand juries were convened, but no indictment was ever handed down. Powerless to find or indict Al, public officials began a campaign of harassment targeting various Capone businesses—all of which simply underscored the futility of the high-profile investigation.

Capone would never enjoy the public immunity he had owned in previous years.

Capone Retreats, Then Returns

Remarkably, Capone remained at large for nearly four months—initially hiding out with friends in the outlying community of Chicago Heights. He then put even more distance between himself and Chicago, retreating 200 miles away to Lansing, Michigan, home to a vibrant Italian-American community, a number of whom had relocated from Chicago. At first keeping a very low profile near a lake outside of Lansing, Capone over the months came out of the shadows and became a visible if discreet presence in Lansing—well-known in the Italian community, and even among public officials and police. Those who knew him during this period invariably describe him as well-dressed, polite, and generous with the community. It appears he took stock of his life at this point, and made a decision to try to reinvent himself as a respectable businessman.

Knowing he couldn't run forever, Capone began a series of unofficial long-distance negotiations with Chicago law enforcement, and in late July of 1926 returned to Chicago and turned himself in. It was a risky move, and Capone casually asserted his innocence to anyone who would listen, describing the murdered McSwiggin as a friend, and even bragging that he was on the Capone payroll. The gamble paid off when the judge quickly dismissed the case for lack of evidence.

Capone was back in business.

Another Murder, Then Peace

While Capone was intent on attaining respectability and distancing himself from his image as a gangster, the longstanding feud with Hymie Weiss continued to fester. The two sides traded attacks, with Capone miraculously escaping a spectacular armed assault on the Hawthorne Hotel in Cicero. On September 20, 1926, North Side gang assailants riding in a motorcade of ten vehicles sprayed gunfire from tommy guns and shotguns at Capone while he was dining in a restaurant on the first floor. Capone was saved by bodyguard, Frankie Rio, who threw him to the ground immediately, but bullets and flying glass injured many innocent bystanders. Since he was the target, Capone paid for the medical care of some of the victims, and shaken by the nearly successful attempt, which he correctly assumed was the work of the North Side, he decided to attempt to negotiate a truce.

Despite Capone's entreaties, Bugs Moran and Hymie Weiss would have none of it unless Capone had John Scalise and Albert Anselmi (who were responsible for Dion O'Banion's hit) killed. Thus, Capone concocted a fool-proof plan. At 4:00 on the afternoon of October 11, 1926, Hymie Weiss and some of his men headed for their headquarters, the old Schofield flower shop. After parking their cars and walking toward the building, two gunmen who were hidden nearby opened fire on the group with a submachine gun and a shotgun, mortally wounding Weiss and killing one of his associates. There was considerable speculation about Capone's role in the killing, but no charges were filed. Capone had just eliminated one of his mortal enemies.

With Weiss out of the picture, Capone made another bold and audacious move: hosting a "peace conference" designed to produce a lasting peace between Chicago's rival gangs. In classic Capone style, he made no attempt to disguise the nature of the meeting or its participants, and held it in full public view at a hotel near City Hall and across the street from the office of the chief of police. Former Mayor "Big Bill" Thompson, seeking a political comeback, was asked to preside and accepted. The meeting was a success and a "general amnesty" was agreed upon. For 70 days afterward, there wasn't a single murder connected with bootlegging, the longest stretch of peace since the start of Prohibition. Publicly, Capone even spoke of retiring.

Capone Riding High

Discredited by the fiasco of the McSwiggin investigation, William Dever was ousted from the mayor's office and replaced in early 1927 by his old foe "Big Bill" Thompson. With the amiable and lax Thompson back in office, Capone emerged from his unofficial retirement and assumed a more visible public role than ever. His headquarters at the Metropole expanded to fifty rooms, nearly the entire hotel, and was the site of non-stop drinking and gambling and prostitution. Capone was seen prominently at a wide range of sporting events, especially Cubs games, and was a member of the official delegation greeting Charles Lindbergh after his successful transatlantic flight. He hosted a huge public party following the much-anticipated heavyweight rematch between Jack Dempsey and Gene Tunney, and he even conducted the band he had hired as it played Gershwin's "Rhapsody in Blue."

The year 1927 saw the Capone organization's income hit new highs—over $100 million by some estimates. A brief stretch of violence broke out as Capone skirmished with an up-and-coming rival, Joseph Aiello, trying to move in on the always hotly contested North Side territory. But a few months later, fearing for his life, Aiello and his two brothers fled town. Capone held a press conference and brazenly announced, "I'm the boss. I'm going to continue to run things."[7]

Aiello

Chapter 6: The Beginning of the End

Though Al Capone appeared to be on top of the world at the close of 1927, the elements of his downfall were starting to fall into place. While Chicago Mayor "Big Bill" Thompson was content to look the other way, a new breed of law enforcement officials had no such patience for business as usual. Among these was a new chief of police, Mike Hughes, who promised a crackdown on gangs and hundreds of new cops on the street. Angered by this new policy, and

---

[7] Bergreen, p. 239

not trusting or respecting Thompson, Capone impulsively announced he was retiring from the Chicago scene—and this time seemed to really mean it. In a long, rambling, self-pitying monologue to the press, Capone declared he was heading to Florida at the end of the year. "Let the worthy citizens of Chicago get their liquor the best they can. I'm sick of the job. It's a thankless one and full of grief."[8]

In early December, Capone indeed boarded a train—but for Los Angeles and not Florida. Much to his surprise, he was treated coldly there. The chief of police told him he was not welcome and gave him 12 hours to leave. Though he ended up staying a few days longer, Capone was soon back on a train to Illinois. Back in Chicago, Hughes had announced an ambitious plan to put all gangsters under arrest. Capone got off the train early, in Joliet, only to be arrested there and quickly released.

Soon after New Year's, Capone finally did head to Florida, to the city of Miami. Though public officials there also expressed mixed feelings about Capone's presence, the city, which had been devastated by a hurricane the previous year, was badly in need of new investment, and privately the mayor arranged for Capone to buy an expensive villa on Palm Island through an intermediary. As hard as he fought for social respectability in Miami, it continually eluded him. The details of his real estate transaction eventually were made public, and though Capone and later his wife remained in the villa for years (after spending most of the 1930s in jail, Capone would return there to die), he was never truly accepted, and his presence there was always considered an embarrassment.

Capone's New Adversaries

Though the new Chicago chief of police succeeded at times in making life difficult for Capone, it was three other officials who were ultimately instrumental in bringing him down. By 1928, Capone was so powerful that the president of the Chicago Crime Commission had to ask his permission and assistance to hold an honest presidential election. Though Capone came through, the new president, Herbert Hoover, was not so grateful that he would not try to put him out of business. The plan was to prosecute the gangster on both tax evasion and Prohibition violations. Ness was chosen to lead the anti-liquor team.

Still just in his mid-20s, Ness was chosen not for his skill but for his reputation for honesty. According to some estimates, the profits from nearly one-third of 100 barrels of beer produced in Chicago each day went to pay off corrupt cops and political officials. That made choosing a team of agents rather difficult. However, after poring over reams of personnel records, Ness whittled a list from 50 possibilities to 15 good men to ultimately an initial dream team of nine: investigator Lyle Chapman, former state trooper Tom Friel, agents Barney Cloonan and Martin J.

[8] Bergreen, p. 262

Lahart, former lawyer Bill Gardner, analyst Mike King, expert driver Joe Leeson, wire-tapping expert Paul W. Robsky, and former Sing Sing corrections officer Samuel M. Seager.

According to Ness in his book, *The Untouchables*:

"I ticked off the general qualities I desired: single, no older than thirty, both the mental and physical stamina to work long hours and the courage and ability to use fist or gun and special investigative techniques. I needed a good telephone man, one who could tap a wire with speed and precision. I needed men who were excellent drivers, for much of our success would depend upon how expertly they could trail the mob's cars and trucks... and fresh faces from other divisions who were not known to the Chicago mobsters."

By the time the team was assembled and trained to his standards, Capone and his crew had killed a countless number of men who had tried to get in his way. Still, Ness's principles and love for adventure drove him forward, even if he was still cautious.

"Doubts raced through my mind as I considered the feasibility of enforcing a law which the majority of honest citizens didn't seem to want...Unquestionably, it was going to be highly dangerous. Yet I felt it was quite natural to jump at the task. After all, if you don't like action and excitement, you don't go into police work. And, what the hell, I figured, nobody lives forever!"

True to his personality, Ness jumped into his work with both feet. On the night of their first raid, Ness and his team destroyed 18 stills in the Chicago Heights neighborhood. After having a problem breaking the lock on a Capone brewery, Ness purchased a 10 ton flat-bed truck with a specially designed reinforced steel bumper. When he drove that truck through the door at the next raid, the lock was not a problem. Within six months Capone was out about a million dollars worth of brewery equipment.

Capone's tenure had already proven on occasion that unbearable heat from authorities typically came only after isolated incidents where a law enforcement officer was injured or killed during mob activity. Thus, Capone was nervous about trying to assassinate federally appointed agents by the late '20s, but he always felt perfectly comfortable bribing them. First, Capone offered Ness, who at that time made $3,000 a year, $2,000 a week to back off. When Ness turned him down, he tried to bribe several of his team. They also turned him down cold, leading Ness to publicize their honesty to local newspapers, saying, "Possibly it wasn't too important for the world to know that we couldn't be bought, but I did want Al Capone and every gangster in the city to realize that there were still a few law enforcement agents who couldn't be swerved from their duty." When the newspapers ran the story, they called the team members "The Untouchables."

One of the group's favorite tools at this time was the wiretap. Although he later discovered that Capone was also tapping Ness's phones, the wiretaps still yielded a significant amount of information. One of the most valuable operations that Ness learned about was when Capone re-equipped and planned to reopen one of the breweries that Ness had recently closed. Ness bided his time until all the new equipment was in place and raided the brewery just in time to confiscate everything.

Obviously, Capone was a dangerous enemy, and though he was originally reluctant to risk bringing the weight of the federal government down on his head, he began to believe that eliminating Ness was worth taking that chance. One night, after Ness walked his steady girl, Edna Staley, to her door, he wrote that he saw a suspicious looking car on her deserted street.

"...as I approached to within a few yards of it, there was a bright flash from the front window, and I ducked instinctively as my windshield splintered in tune with the bark of a revolver. Without thinking, I jammed the accelerator to the floor. As my car leaped ahead, there was another flash, and the window of my left rear door was smashed by another slug.

The tires squealed as I hurtled around the next corner...Driving madly, I circled the block, taking my gun from the shoulder holster and holding it in my left hand as I doubled back to get behind the car which had ambushed me. Now I wanted my turn, but the would-be assassin had faded into the night."

Unfortunately, not all of his associates were so lucky. One night he was called to the home of his assistant, Frank Basile, who'd been found murdered.

"Lying there was a lifeless husk which had been Frank Basile! I had expected it, I suppose, and in the course of my career I had often witnessed the ravages of violent death. You think, eventually, that nothing can disturb you and that your nerves are impregnable. Yet, looking down at that familiar face, I realized that death is something to which we never become calloused."

Not surprisingly, Ness wanted to retaliate for Basile's death, but he nevertheless stayed above the law. Instead, he had all the 45 trucks, most of which were brand new, that he had confiscated from Capone polished to a high shine and driven slowly past the mobster's office in parade fashion while Capone was forced to look on.

Of all the people who would bring about Capone's downfall, Ness would become the most famous for his work in the Chicago Prohibition Bureau. His dramatic raids against Capone's bootlegging operations had a higher profile than the tax evasion work, and Ness dramatized his role and the operations of the Untouchables with considerable embellishment.

Ness and Capone will forever be linked, but it was U.S. Attorney George Johnson, the man who hired Ness for the Chicago office, who played a more substantial role in Capone's demise. Johnson saw to it that, for the first time, various agencies coordinated their efforts against Capone at a high level. Perhaps just as important, and working almost entirely out of the limelight, was Treasury Department investigator Frank Wilson, who worked tirelessly for years to compile a case against Capone for tax evasion. More worried about the various murder raps he was associated with, Capone never took the tax evasion charges seriously until it was too late.

Johnson

The raids and work of the Untouchables had forced Capone to cut back on the bribes he paid out because he could no longer afford them. However, clear proof that Ness did not bring down Capone singlehandedly was evidenced by the fact that Capone conducted the most famous gangland hit in American history well after Ness's activities were in full swing.

A Violent Start to 1928

"Big Bill" Thompson's second stay in the mayor's office was just as disastrous as his first. His negligence and incompetence gave organized crime free reign for a while, but it also led to political instability. As an important primary approached in April (one widely viewed as a referendum on his administration), the city was rocked by a series of bombings targeting public officials. With Capone spending much of his time in Miami, there was no one to enforce the peace, and freelancers looking to establish their clout were likely responsible. Election Day itself was a violent and often chaotic affair, but the voters nonetheless rejected many of Thompson's men. Thompson, who had been harboring ambitions for a presidential campaign, began to show less and less interest in the city's daily affairs.

In 1927, Capone had begun to suspect that his old associate (and former boss at the Harvard Club) Frankie Yale was orchestrating hijackings of his own whiskey shipments and then keeping the booze for himself. Capone asked James "Filesy" DeAmato, an old friend, to get to the bottom of things, and DeAmato confirmed Capone's suspicions, reporting that Frankie was hijacking the booze shipments. Shortly after that, DeAmato's cover was blown, leading him to attempt a haphazard attempt on Frankie Yale's life on the night of July 1, 1927. That attempt failed, but the hit on Filesy DeAmato six nights later did not, as DeAmato was gunned down on a Brooklyn street corner.

DeAmato may have failed to kill Yale, but Capone was a bit more experienced in that regard, and when he returned to Miami the next month, Capone began making plans to have Yale assassinated. On July 1, 1928, a year to the date of DeAmato's attempt on his life, Yale received a phone call at one of his clubs informing him that something was wrong with his wife Lucy, who at the time Yale assumed was at home caring for their infant daughter. Not thinking clearly, Yale quickly jumped into his car and sped off, only to notice at a red light that he was being tailed by a Buick with four passengers. After a chase up New Utrecht and onto 44th Street, the Buick's passengers riddled Yale's car with shotguns and submachine guns. Yale's car was outfitted with armor, but his windows were not bullet-proof. Laying dead in his car on a Brooklyn street corner, Yale was wearing a luxurious belt buckle believed to have been given him by Al Capone.

Yale received a huge, opulent funeral with some 100,000 attendees, a reflection of Yale's huge status in the racketeering world. While Yale's gangland funeral set the gold standard for mob funerals, it did not include Capone, who had carefully arranged to be in Miami at the time. Though Capone was never formally connected to Yale's murder, the presence of cars with Chicago plates at the scene of the crime inevitably drew suspicion his way, and the use of tommy guns was a hallmark of Chicago gangland warfare that had previously not been used in New York City. In later years, researchers concluded that Yale's assassins included Capone gunmen Fred "Killer" Burke, Gus Winkler, George "Shotgun" Ziegler, and Louis "Little New York" Campagna, most of whom would participate in the St. Valentine's Day Massacre seven months later. Furthermore, one of the tommy guns used in the St. Valentine's Day Massacre would later be linked by ballistic testing to Yale's murder.

To all outward appearances, Capone was still on top. Later that month he moved his Chicago offices from the Metropole Hotel to the even grander Lexington and had it equipped with a vast menu of safety measures. Capone also made sure that, unlike Yale, his cars were fully protected, and he had his Cadillac fitted with bullet-proof glass, run-flat tires and a police siren. On December 8, 1941, President Franklin Delano Roosevelt rode to the Capitol to deliver his famous

"Infamy" speech the day after Pearl Harbor in a heavily armored 1928 Cadillac 341A Town Sedan. That Cadillac had originally belonged to Al Capone, and it had been impounded after it was confiscated by Treasury Department officials during the investigation of Capone's finances.

As the fall election approached in 1928, Frank Loesch, the head of the Chicago Crime Commission, approached Capone and privately sought his intervention. Capone made sure the police, many of whom were on his payroll, were out in full force, and the election was a peaceful one.

Chapter 7: The St. Valentine's Day Massacre

At the start of 1929, Capone's position appeared secure. A raid spearheaded by the new U.S. attorney George Johnson on his Chicago Heights operations seemed to be only a minor inconvenience at the time — little did Al know that ledgers seized during the raid would prove crucial in the government's tax evasion case. His brother Ralph was not nearly as clever as Al in covering up his financial tracks and would end up being a weak link.

Meanwhile, the never-ending feud with the North Side gangs continued to be a thorn in Capone's side. Bugs Moran, still bitter at Al for the Hymie Weiss hit, had tried repeatedly and unsuccessfully to assassinate him. Having failed so frequently in his attempted hits on Capone, Bugs now decided to go after one of Capone's right-hand men, "Machine Gun" Jack McGurn, a tough-nosed bodyguard who had risen to become a prominent partner in Capone's organization. McGurn was peppered with machine gun spray but somehow survived. After he recovered, he approached Capone with an ambitious plan to take out the entire Moran gang once and for all.

Machine Gun Jack McGurn

The scheme took weeks to put together, and involved dangling a cheap new supply of quality whiskey, with the intention of luring Bugs Moran to the SMC Cartage warehouse on North Clark

Street. Moran took the bait, and on the morning of February 14, 1929, a bunch of Moran's crew turned up at the warehouse to wait for the shipment. At about 10:30, a car full of what appeared to be policemen pulled up to the garage where the drop was to take place. Thinking it was one of many sham raids in which the cops simply went through the motions and were really just after a bigger bribe, Moran's men let their guard down, dropped their guns and put their hands up. The "policemen" were in fact McGurn and his hand-picked crew, which mostly consisted of out-of-towners that Capone figured none of the North Side men would recognize.

Fortunately for Bugs Moran, he was running late to the warehouse, and as he and Ted Newberry headed toward the rear of the warehouse, they saw the police car pull up. Naturally, Moran and Newberry turned around and fled, at which point they ran into Henry Gusenberg and warned him to stay away. Another Moran associate, Willie Marks, spotted the police car and hid, making sure to take down the car's license plate number before fleeing.

With two of the "officers" having lined up the 7 men present against the rear wall of the garage, it seems that one of Moran's men, Albert Weinshank, was mistaken for Moran himself, a result of the fact that they were similar in size and stature and dressed similarly. Witnesses later explained that they saw four men, two dressed as cops, walk into the warehouse. Likely believing Weinshank was Bugs Moran, the two "cops" gave the signal to the pair in civilian clothes, and those two opened fire with tommy guns, ruthlessly slaughtering the defenseless men. For good measure, the bodies were also shot with shotguns, which all but blew off the faces of John May and James Clark. And to keep the ruse going, the four men emerged from the warehouse with the two "cops" escorting the two "civilians" with their hands up.

The St. Valentine's Day Massacre

As Capone's men fled the scene, one of the survivors began piping up: Highball, John May's German Shepherd. With the dog barking, bystanders and eventually authorities discovered the grisly scene, and somehow Frank Gusenberg was still alive. In fact, despite suffering 14 bullet wounds, he was still conscious. A famous legend is that as Gusenberg lay dying from the gunshot wounds, he told police that nobody shot him. Though this statement is probably apocryphal, nobody opened their mouths, and nobody was ever convicted for the "Saint Valentine's Day Massacre," the most famous gangland hit in American history, although Capone's involvement is unquestioned. It is widely believed that the 4 gunmen were Jack McGurn, John Scalise, Albert Anselmi, and Frank Rio, the bodyguard who had saved Capone from Moran's assassination attempt in 1926.

Scalise

It was a spectacular and notorious hit, but in many ways it backfired on Capone. The crew thought they had got Moran, but Bugs was in fact late for the meeting and had narrowly escaped. Though no one was ever charged or arrested, ballistics evidence linked McGurn to the crime and inevitably fingers started pointing toward Al. It was a black mark for the city of Chicago, and the national press produced a stream of sensational articles profiling Capone and his reign of terror in Chicago. The story even caught the eye of President Hoover, who began putting pressure on federal authorities to take action.

Chapter 8: Capone's Downfall

For awhile, Capone delighted in this new wave of notoriety, but he made a series of miscues that helped hasten his downfall. The growing pressure to do something about Capone led the Chicago U.S. Attorney George Johnson to issue a subpoena ordering him to appear before a federal grand jury on March 12. Capone delayed and feigned sickness. Though he ultimately showed up a week later, investigators were able to prove he was not in fact ill, opening him up to a contempt of court charge. But all the while Capone carried himself with his characteristic bravado, assuming he would again find a way to escape charges.

Released at the moment from further questioning, it has been widely speculated that Capone returned to Chicago to discover that two of the gunmen who had been part of the St. Valentine's Day Massacre, Scalise and Anselmi, were seeking to turn on him and align themselves with fellow Sicilian Joseph Guinta, who had secretly formed an anti-Capone alliance with Joe Aiello (who Al had sent packing several years earlier). Capone threw an elaborate banquet for Guinta and the two gunmen—and after hours of food and drink turned on the three men with a baseball bat (a scene immortalized in the movie *The Untouchables*). It is believed that while Capone nearly beat them to death, he handed off the task of murdering them to his associates. The following day, the completely disfigured bodies of Scalise, Anselmi, and Joseph Giunta were discovered on a road near Hammond, Indiana. It was at first assumed that the North Side Gang had killed them in retaliation for the St. Valentine's Day Massacre, at least until it was discovered that the three men had been lured to a banquet with their Sicilian friends, making it far more likely that it was an inside job by Capone.

By now, even within the national community of racketeers and organized crime, Capone, with his increasingly volatile behavior and the attention he was drawing from federal authorities, was seen as a liability. That May, at a gathering in Atlantic City, a national Commission of racketeers presented him with a proposal that essentially involved the gradual dismantling of his empire for the good of all. The Commission was headed by none other than Al's old mentor, Johnny Torrio, unexpectedly emerged from retirement.

With the organized crime world now against him, and a target on his back from the federal government, Bugs Moran and countless other enemies, Capone seems to have panicked. He concocted a bizarre (but for the moment effective) scheme to have himself arrested in Philadelphia on a concealed weapons charge. And on May 18, 1929, Capone began a projected year-long sentence in a local county jail. He had, for now at least, avoided the day of reckoning.

Al Capone's cell at the Eastern State Penitentiary in Philadelphia

Al's scheme threw law enforcement officials a bit of a curveball, but they continued to build their case against him, targeting brother Ralph as the weak link in the Capone organization. In what was seen as a test case in the new strategy, Ralph was arrested for tax evasion in early October. He was released on bail, with the trial set for May. But Ralph was sloppy and continued to provide the government with evidence gathered through law enforcement's latest technique of wire-tapping. Ness monitored Ralph's every move and conversation, and he led a series of dramatic raids on the Capones' operations.

When Al Capone was finally released from a Pennsylvania prison on March 17, 1930 (two months early for good behavior), the world had changed. In October of the previous year, the stock market had crashed, sending the economy into a tailspin. In less than six months the number of unemployed had nearly doubled. The Roaring Twenties were over, and the nation was in a somber and sober mood. Though Capone's release landed him on the cover of *Time* magazine, he was no longer the folk hero he had once been. Frank Loesch of the Chicago Crime Commission, who Al had never taken seriously, developed an ingenious new media strategy by issuing a Public Enemies list, with Capone of course at Number 1. The idea was later adapted by J. Edgar Hoover for the FBI's Most Wanted list. The tide had turned. The Commission had formed in 1919 among civic leaders aiming to work with the public to stop organized crime in the city. In addition to lobbying, the Commission put together records detailing organized crime in Chicago that were even better than the police had.

In April 1930, Ralph stood trial for tax evasion and was quickly convicted. The government began pursuing other Capone associates, including Al's old friend Jack Guzik. Emboldened by the shift in public opinion and the new Public Enemy campaign, officials in Miami took aim at Al, threatening to arrest him on vague vagrancy charges or have his Palm Island villa declared a public nuisance. Public officials elsewhere followed suit, and though nothing came of it, Capone could not escape the nagging fear that the government was out to get him.

As the tax evasion cases against many of his friends went forward, Al tried his best to hold on. In November he opened up his own soup kitchen, feeding over 5,000 on Thanksgiving alone. In December his baby sister Mafalda was married and Al threw her a grand party. Though his brother and associates were going to jail, it was clear the government was having a tough time assembling a case against him. 1930 came to a close and he was still a free and powerful and rich man.

However, all throughout this time Frank Wilson, the Treasury investigator targeting Capone, was making slow but sure progress, succeeding in placing a double agent in Capone's organization and in "turning" a couple of former associates. Ness received all the headlines in the spring of 1931, but it was the June 5 indictment charging Al with 22 counts of tax evasion that was to be the backbreaker. Even then, Capone still had some tricks up his sleeve. He first attempted to make a plea deal, but after the judge warned he might not follow prosecutors' sentencing recommendations as part of that deal, Capone withdrew the guilty plea. He then plotted to bribe and intimidate potential jurors, but this was discovered by Ness and the Untouchables, who had the jury pool switched. Capone's luck had run out.

At the October trial Capone was convicted of only five counts, but that was enough to warrant an 11 year sentence at the Federal Penitentiary in Georgia. Eliot Ness personally put him on the train to Atlanta, and by the end of the month, Public Enemy Number 1 was in a Cook County Jail.

Capone in Prison

For a while, Al held out hope he would once more be able to wiggle out of his troubles. His brother Ralph had been sentenced to three years in federal prison, but was still at large while his lawyers filed appeals (though those appeals finally ran out in November). Meanwhile, the still formidable Capone set up shop at the county jail, made sure he had access to good food and even liquor, and continued to conduct business as usual. In the spring of 1932, with his legal team still filing appeals, Capone engaged in a last-ditch publicity stunt, offering to help find the kidnapped and missing son of Charles Lindbergh if he was released. But in May, Al's final appeal was denied, and he was shipped off to the Atlanta Penitentiary.

In Atlanta, Capone's health went into a long and steady decline, even as he engaged in ongoing legal maneuvers to attain an early release. Resentment over his special treatment in the Cook County Jail led to similar charges in Atlanta, not to mention the fact that he was widely suspected of continuing to carry out the Outfit's criminal enterprises from jail. Thus, in August of 1934 Capone was transferred to the recently opened federal facility of Alcatraz. His neurosyphilis began taking a toll on his mental as well as physical state, and, stripped of his old status and prestige, Al became a target of other prisoners and in 1936 was the object of a brutal stabbing attack. Two years later he suffered a serious mental breakdown and spent months in the prison hospital.

"The Rock", Alcatraz Island

Capone's cell in Alcatraz

When he was finally released in November of 1939, Capone was a broken man. His family sought experimental treatment for his syphilis at Johns Hopkins, which at best bought him some time. After four months he was released and traveled to his Palm Island Villa to live out his remaining years. He received visits from family and old associates, all monitored closely by the FBI. The visitors made small talk with Al, but he was not his old lucid self and was at times delusional, rambling at length about Communists and old foe Bugs Moran. Mental evaluations concluded that Capone had devolved into the mental ability of a 12 year old.

In 1945 he was one of the first civilians to be treated for syphilis with penicillin, but his health slowly but surely gave out, and on January 25 1947, just a week after his 48th birthday, Al "Scarface" Capone passed away after a stroke and cardiac arrest.

Chapter 9: Cleaning Up Cleveland

It's no surprise that the highlights of Ness's life were his activities against Al Capone, but he was still just 28 years old when Capone was sent to jail for good. Riding high on the wave of his success in Chicago, Ness was promoted to Chief Investigator of the Prohibition Bureau for Chicago. In that capacity he finished mopping up the rest of the "small fry" operators that remained after Capone was shut down.

After Prohibition ended in 1933, he was transferred to head the Ohio office, where his primary task was very different. Ness had to track down and arrest moonshiners in the Appalachian mountains of Kentucky, Tennessee and southern Ohio. Within a few days he staged the first in a series of attacks on local bootleggers that would soon grow to an average of one still closed each day. Within a year, there were no significant illegal stills left in the area.

In November of 1935, Harold Burton was elected mayor of Cleveland on a "law and order" ticket. Word went out that he was looking for a new Safety Director to come in and clean up corruption in the city's police and fire departments. When he heard about the job, Ness knew it was for him. However, there were a few things standing in his way. First, Ness had no interest in politics, and Burton was known for being thoroughly Republican, leaving Ness to wonder if he could work well in such a politically charged environment. Also, there was the matter of his age. Though he had already accomplished more than most men in his situation would in a lifetime, Ness was still only 33 years old. Finally, he was not even from Cleveland and had only lived there about a year.

Mayor Burton

While these handicaps may have made most men a dark horse at best for the position, Ness went to work campaigning for the position. Working with a reporter friend, he contacted everyone he could think of who knew him and would recommend him to the mayor. Because many of these men were business owners who had previously been harassed by mob connections, they were very enthusiastic about having someone with an unimpeachable reputation come in and clean up the city.

Following a brief interview in December, Mayor Burton offered Ness the position of Safety Director for Cleveland. According to sources close to the mayor, everyone that heard that Ness had applied for the position insisted that he was the only man for the job. He went to work the day after his interview.

Ness as Safety Director

When reporters asked Ness about his plans for dealing with the corruption in the Safety Department, Ness assured them that no one would be punished without an ample investigation. However, he also emphasized that once he had made up his mind that someone needed to be removed, the press would not know about it until after the fact. The family of even the worst cop deserved better than to learn about his indictment in the papers.

In spite of this road block, the press still loved Ness. One editorial glowed, "If any man knows the inside of the crime situation here, his name is Ness. The mere announcement of his selection is worth a squadron of police in the effect it will have on the underworld's peace of mind."

Of course, the men who would be working for Ness were not so enthusiastic. In addition to corruption, both the police and fire departments suffered from a general malaise brought about by lack of discipline and training. This showed not only in their lives, but also in their uniforms, as police were often seen on the streets in sloppy, unbuttoned uniforms and dirty shoes. Worse than that, they were also seen in bars in the same uniforms.

Many of their concerns about Ness disappeared when they met him. Having heard tales of his daring exploits against Capone, they expected a larger than life macho man with wide shoulders and a booming voice. Instead, they met a quiet, well groomed gentleman who still preferred books to sports and quiet conversation to loud quarrels. When asked about the police attitude toward their new boss, one reporter commented, "Listen, you don't get any real reaction out of police at a time like this. They have seen safety directors come and go and things don't usually change much under the surface. Most safety directors don't mean anything to cops. A police department is nothing but a set of vegetables. You don't get sharp reactions from vegetables."

The force veterans, some of whom were nearly old enough to be his father, relaxed and announced to their buddies that the "Boy Scout" would be no trouble. Of course, they were soon proven dead wrong. Ness came into office with a plan to reward good work and punish corruption and soon implemented the same types of wire taps that he used in Chicago against Capone to gather evidence against the men he suspected of wrongdoing. Most of all, he let everyone know that they could not deceive him, telling reporters, "I am not going to be a remote director. I am going to be out, and I'll cover this town pretty well."

As soon as the Christmas holidays were over, Ness began touring every precinct in town. He met the commanding officers and toured their stations, asking question not just about what was wrong but also about what was right. He made careful notes about who needed new equipment and which areas could stand to tighten up their appearances, and he made sure to let every man know that he had an open door policy. Anyone could come speak to him about any concern they had. However, out of respect for the chain of command, he would have to go through his own chief, who in turn could not stand in the way of any meeting.

In addition to corruption within his own ranks, Ness also had to deal with organized crime and gambling, which were making the city miserable. While he personally did not see gambling as a sin, he did see breaking the laws prohibiting gambling as evil behavior that had to be stopped.

"It is debatable, whether gambling is morally wrong, but from the policing standpoint I have an entirely different picture. Gambling brings into financial power men recognized as law violators. They collect large sums of money, which must be distributed among many people, some of them public officials. Gradually, with their money, they make inroads into the police departments and the courts."

One of the most egregious gambling parlors was the Harvard Club, located outside Ness's jurisdiction in the Cleveland suburbs. The Sheriff in charge of policing that part of the county had no interest in shutting the place down, especially since he received a regular income from the owners in the form of bribes. However, county prosecutor Frank Cullitan had other ideas and appealed to Ness for help.

When Ness went to Mayor Burton to obtain his permission to assist Cullitan in breaking up the Harvard Club, he ran headlong into his first political battle. Cullitan was a Democrat and had supported Burton's opponent in the recent election. Therefore Burton had no interest in helping him do anything, even if it was closing down a blatantly illegal gambling club.

Unable to take his men across the city limits officially, Ness went as a private citizen and persuaded many members of the police force to go with him to help with a raid on the club. He also called his friends at the local papers and invited them to come cover a story about how Cleveland police had to go out into the county to help an honest prosecutor serve warrants that the Sheriff wanted no part of.

When Ness pulled into the parking lot of the Harvard Club where Cullitan and the few constables he'd been able to bring with him were hovering in the cold, he was at the head of a police army that included 29 patrolmen, 4 plainclothes officers and 10 motorcycle cops. Everyone there was armed to the teeth, except Ness. Still, after a brief consultation with Cullitan, he led the way to the action, banging on the door with a borrowed nightstick and announcing who he was and that he was coming in to serve warrants on those present.

When the door swung open, Ness found himself face to face with five thugs wielding machine guns. However, seeing the forces behind him, they chose not to fire. Instead, they laid their weapons down as Ness stood back and let Cullitan execute his own plan. He went in last, letting Cullitan bask in what all expected to be a moment of glory.

Unfortunately, it was not. Instead, those who had risked their lives for justice found a cavernous, nearly empty room, though they were able to confiscate a few blackjack tables as well as the race board still hanging on the wall. They also arrested a total of 20 gangsters who had remained behind, perhaps in hopes of mowing down a few cops. Instead, they were carried off in handcuffs as Ness and Cullitan congratulated each other for a job well done and flashing cameras recorded the beginning of the end of organized crime in Cleveland.

One of the side effects of corruption in the police force was the low morale it led to among the officers. Those who were incompetent but politically well-connected were often promoted over those who were skilled but only interested in doing a good job. In fact, in some precincts, doing a good job could get an officer labeled a troublemaker and lead to harassment from his superiors.

Speaking out to local businessmen, Ness observed, "In any city where corruption continues, it follows that some officials are playing ball with the underworld. If politicians are committed to a program of 'protection,' police work becomes exceedingly difficult, and the officer on the beat, being discouraged from his duty, decides it is best to see as little crime as possible."

In Ness's mind, the perfect cop was part student, part athlete and part diplomat. Anything less was unacceptable. To drive this point home, he soon fired Michael Corrigan and Joseph Dunne for drinking while on duty and overall poor behavior. A few days later, he transferred 122 officers to new duty stations in order to break up cliques, and he also demoted crooked cops. He took this opportunity to promote some officers with stellar reputations. Finally, he transferred the questionably competent head of the Detective Bureau, Emmet Potts, to Traffic Division and replaced him with his own Deputy Inspector, Joseph Sweeney. *The Cleveland Press* heartily approved of this change, reporting, "Sweeney is one of the ablest officers in the Cleveland Police Department and has scrupulously held aloof from political activity and factional disputes within the department. Eliot Ness was at pains in discussing Potts' reassignment to spare him humiliation. For the problem in dealing with officers like Potts is not finding ways to humiliate them, but finding ways to get out of them the service of which they are capable, while at the same time curing them of the tendencies that have limited their effectiveness in the past."

One of the things that stood in the way of Ness's work against internal corruption was police loyalty. Even honest officers were reluctant to report on others who weren't. Ness took a four pronged approach to combating this problem.

1. He hired a new team of Untouchables who were from outside the Cleveland police force and had no friends in the department. He even paid them through a secret fund so that no one would know how much they made. They became known as the "Secret Six."
2. Ness recognized and promoted young men in the department who were honest and well educated, as well as seasoned veterans like David Cowles, head of the crime lab, and James Limber, one of his best gambling fighters.
3. Ness went out into the streets himself, getting to know members of the local underworld who would, in turn, let him know who was on the take and who was honest.
4. He used his connections in the press to find out who had a bad reputation and why, as well as who was paying cops to look the other way.

It was from this last source that Ness learned about a police captain, Louis Cadek, who was so corrupt that he had been transferred 28 times over his 30 year career. Though he had only earned a total salary of $68,000 during his lifetime, in 1935 he had over $100,000 in the bank. Needless to say, Cadek soon found himself out of a job and in hot water.

In an effort to attract and train new, competent men to replace those he was weeding out, Ness created the first Cleveland Police Academy. There potential officers would learn the latest method for handling everything from gathering evidence to giving testimony in court. Those who made it through the academy would still have to pass tough civil service exams, as well as an oral board. Finally, he insisted that every applicant pass a thorough background check before he made it to the streets.

One of the positive side effects of a new and better police department was a positive increase in city morale. During the early years of the Depression, Cleveland had become known as a dirty, crime-ridden city that no one would live in unless they had to. Certainly no tourist would ever visit. However, as the national press began reporting about the work of the famous Eliot Ness in cleaning up crime and restoring order, people became more open to visiting Cleveland and even holding conventions there. This stimulated the economy, providing more jobs and raising the standard of living, and before long, people were actually speaking of Cleveland with smiles instead of grimaces.

Chapter 10: The Cleveland Torso Murderer

The first major sign of Cleveland's new and improved status was the Republican National Convention, which held in the city in the early summer of 1936. Of course Mayor Burton was at every event, shaking hands and welcoming dignitaries from around the country to his fair city. Fortunately, with all the attention on the politicians, no one noticed right away that Eliot Ness and many of his ablest men looked distracted and concerned.

A few month before Ness had been appointed Safety Director, two men had been found decapitated near a ravine in a seedy part of Cleveland. At first, police believed the incident to be related to a romantic quarrel and treated it as a regular homicide. When a down and out prostitute was found in January of 1936, also decapitated but with her arms and legs removed too, they still didn't see a clear connection. However, when another decapitated body was found during the week of the Republican National Convention, Ness and his head of homicide, Sergeant James Hogan, began to believe there was a pattern emerging.

While Ness assured Hogan that he had no intention of getting involved with the case personally, he also let the Sergeant know that he wanted nothing said to the press, especially while the Convention was in town. He was also planning for another big event, the Great Lakes Exposition, a sort of smaller version of the World's Fair. In addition to coordinating security and a strong police presence, Ness was also preparing his own exhibit on behalf of the Cleveland Police force. Showcasing the latest in their criminal procedures, he hoped to show the world what could be accomplished by honest, well-trained men who were committed to fighting crime.

Another issue on his mind was the Blackhawk Inn. According to Cleveland Councilman Anton Vehovec, the Inn was not so much a restaurant as a front for illegal gambling. Vehovec also claimed that the reason it had not been shut down was that the police captain for the precinct was himself involved in the gambling.

A few days later, Ness raided the Inn. While he was confiscating betting slips and making arrests, the owner of the restaurant, Eddie Harwood walked in and declared they couldn't make any trouble for him because his father, Police Captain Michael Harwood, "runs this district." "Well, well," Ness is reported to have said, "I'm Eliot Ness and I run the police department in this whole town." While nothing could be proven against Eddie, Captain Harwood was immediately suspended pending a full investigation. Ness told reporters, "The matter has now gone far beyond the operation of a single bookmaking establishment. It is a question of police efficiency, discipline and honesty in the Fourteenth Precinct, and every officer in it is going to be called on for a recital of everything going on in that precinct." By the time the investigation was complete, Ness had amassed enough evidence to summarily fire Harwood.

Ness's next target was a betting hall called McGinty's. According to reports from several undercover officers, the owner regularly bribed police officers to stay away from his business and to warn him of any planned raids. The head of the precinct, Captain Adolph Lenahan, had allowed the gambling to continue unmolested for more than 10 years.

When Ness called Lenahan in for a meeting, the chief showed up drunk, resulting in his immediate suspension. Ness then carried out a well-planned, secret raid that garnered him all the evidence he'd need to prosecute the seven employees and 80 customers he arrested. In the meantime, Lenahan retired in order to save his pension. With men around them being suspended right and left, the remaining officers tightened up on their activities, running regular raids that closed down dozens of gambling joints across town.

Part of Ness's success lay in the mystery that surrounded him. He mingled equally well with high ranking politicians and criminal lowlifes. He demanded the best from others and never gave anything less himself. When dealing with those whom he believed to be honest or helpful, he was quiet and polite to a fault. However, when rushing into a gambling joint or chewing out a dirty cop, he was a raving tyrant. And no matter who a reporter talked to in Cleveland, nobody would claim to know Ness well.

Still, Ness could be almost unreasonably kind when he felt it was called for. He retained the Chief of Police, Matowitz, because even though he was not very good at his job, he was honest and hardworking. Ness also took time out of his busy schedule to personally swear in new rookie officers, often giving them a similar version of this speech:

"You have been appointed to this job on your own merits and because you stood at the top of the civil service lists. If anyone says he was responsible for your appointment, ignore him. Your advancement in this department is completely up to you. You are expected to be honest so don't be obligated to anyone, even in small things. When you walk into a restaurant for a meal, pay for it. When you get any marketable commodity useful to you, pay for it. If people want to give you something without charge, you can conclude they are buying your badge and your uniform."

With his internal problems under control and his officers doing a better job shutting down gambling joints, Ness went after a new enemy, extortion and racketeering in the local wholesale food industry. He soon gathered enough evidence to convince local businesses to come forward and testify against "unions" that demanded kick-backs from farmers and truckers who wanted to unload their wares in at the Northern Ohio Food Terminal in Cleveland.

While Ness was focusing most of his attention on organized crime, his men continued to investigate the work of the serial killer they would nickname "the Mad Butcher." In September, another unidentified body was found in the Kingbury Run ravine, making a total of six victims who had been decapitated. Ness assigned 20 detectives to the case to sift through facts, speculation and evidence.

The public terror over the crimes was only made worse by newspaper articles, which naturally included sensationalized reporting:

"Of all the horrible nightmares come to life, the most shuddering is the fiend who decapitates his victims in the dark, dank recesses of Kingsbury Run. That a man of this nature should be permitted to work his crazed vengeance upon six people in a city the size of Cleveland should be the city's shame. No Edgar Allan Poe in his deepest, opium-maddened dream could conceive horror so painstakingly worked out..."

Under pressure from both above and below, Ness did what he did best: he assembled a team of the best men in each field related to the investigation and gave them his complete support. Among those assembled, none stood out like Peter Merylo, a true eccentric and longtime member of the police force. Merylo was obsessed with solving the case and would leave no stone unturned in finding the killer.

In the midst of his frustration over the unsolved murders, Ness at least had the comfort of his biggest anti-corruption success to date. On October 5, 1936, he delivered a stack of evidence to the county prosecutor against 20 formerly high ranking officials from the police department. According to *The Cleveland Press*:

"Out of the wealth of testimony which Director Ness and *The Cleveland Press* accumulated, one salient fact emerges: that the corruption uncovered stems from higher circles than the police department: that the rank and file who have taken money were in many cases the victims of an evil system. In short, the department has been so controlled for the last 20 years that it could not breed or attract men of high character.... young men coming into the department got off to a bad start by having to pay several hundred dollars for the good jobs: anywhere from $500 to $750 for a sergeancy, more for a lieutenancy and as much as $5000 for a captaincy."

As the corrupt cops were eliminated, the better ones rose to the top. Rookie cops made large busts while veterans were finally able to earn much deserved promotions. This in turn strengthened the war on racketeering, as local businessmen came to believe that the police really would protect them against retaliation from the street thugs they reported. Ness urged them on in speeches:

"Gangsters and racketeers could be run out of Cleveland in a few weeks if industrialists and businessmen would report threats and protection schemes. Come in and give me the information. I shall not put you on the spot or expose you on the witness stand. But don't hide the facts and help gangs prosper while injuring yourself and endangering all other decent businesses."

Still, it seemed to Ness that every time he got one aspect of his work under control, another problem would emerge. In February of 1937, the Mad Butcher's seventh decapitated victim washed up near 156th Street. This time it was again the body of a woman, as was the next victim, found a few months later. A ninth body, this time a male, was found a month later, on July 6, 1937.

Around this time the team questioned their first serious suspect. Dr. Frank Sweeney was tall, strong and a well-trained surgeon. He was also an alcoholic and had suffered a serious head trauma during World War I. He also grew up near Kingsbury Run and was very familiar with the area. He had lost his medical license the previous year and was often hospitalized for his addiction. While the investigators originally thought this gave him an alibi, they later learned that the hospital where he stayed had an open campus policy and he was allowed to come and go as he pleased.

Dr. Sweeny would probably have been arrested early in the investigation had it not been for the intervention of his cousin, the powerful U. S. Congressman from Ohio, Martin L Sweeney. Congressman Sweeny constantly berated both Ness and the mayor for wasting their time questioning his cousin and fighting organized crime when there was a mad murderer on the loose.

Congressman Sweeney

Ness could not focus all his attention on just one crime, no matter how heinous, and the police had a new problem dealing with trade unions. There were a series of strikes in Cleveland at the Corrigan-McKinney Mill of Republic Steel, and to cope with both the strikers and those crossing the picket line, Ness ordered his men to have special training in dealing peacefully with volatile situations, saying, "The handling of strikes has so many ramifications that it easily becomes a specialty. Most strikes are similar and one man can soon educate himself in all the things he needs to know."

While working with the labor unions to make the strikes manageable, Ness was able to create some alliances that helped him continue to weed out bad eggs who might try to exploit local business owners. As the city began to get back on its economic feet, the local papers praised his efforts:

"Capital has been driven out of Cleveland because those who wished to spend it here came to believe that racketeering spokesmen for the unions must either be bought off or fought openly with slight chance of victory. Building projects partly completed have been held up by lawless demand of union representatives, by threats to 'pull' the job, by fake jurisdictional claims, etc. Those who furnish the capital are grossly penalized."

Meanwhile, another female victim of the Mad Butcher was discovered in the Cuyahoga River, bringing the total number of dead to 10. Ness assigned a young rookie cop, Thomas Whelan, to tail Sweeny. Though he was soon discovered by his suspect, Whelan continued to follow the doctor, often under very unusual circumstances, for weeks. Nonetheless, two more bodies turned up in mid-April, 1938.

By this time public outcry had risen to such a pitch that Ness felt he must take some sort of action. Thus, on the night of April 18, he raided the shantytown in Kingsbury Run and rousted out all the homeless men living there. He sent most to the precinct house, where they were fingerprinted and released. To ensure that they could not again return to their makeshift location, he torched the whole area, burning it to the ground.

Much to his surprise, the public was not pleased with the way the police had approached a group of innocent men and driven them from their homes. They wanted real action, and the killer caught, not hobos harassed. Dismayed and confused, Ness took one final step toward solving the case.

On August 23, 1938, Ness had premier polygraph expert Leonard Keeler come from Chicago with one of the new lie detectors. Keeler administered the test to Sweeney in a Cleveland hotel suite, and assured Ness that the doctor was indeed the Mad Butcher. Just to be sure, Ness had him repeat the test. Still, he came to the same conclusions. However, with no hard evidence to go on, there was still no way to prosecute him.

Then, the unexpected happened. Sweeny once more checked himself into the local mental hospital two days later. He would remain voluntarily committed for the rest of his life. Though he could come and go as he pleased, hospital personnel were told to alert the Cleveland police anytime he left hospital property.

The Mad Butcher never killed again, but no one was ever arrested or prosecuted for the crimes.

Chapter 11: Unsalvageable

While Ness's career continued to prosper, his personal life was a mess. In 1938, his wife of nine years, Edna, filed for divorce, seemingly having grown tired of sitting home alone while he was out chasing bad guys. She returned to Chicago, while Ness began to spend more and more of his off duty time at local bars and wild parties, often in the company of a number of different women. The conservative, hard-working people of Cleveland were not amused.

Perhaps hoping to regain some lost glory, Ness tried to recreate himself once more into the prosecutor of organized crime. In fall of 1938 he successfully shut down the Mayfield Road Mob, arresting a total 23 gangsters and sending them to prison.

Next, hoping to appeal to the public's concern about vehicular safety, he reorganized the Cleveland Traffic Bureau from the graveyard for misfits to a respected part of the police department. He staffed it with well-trained officers and put an end to ticket fixing and ignoring bench warrants. He also created the Accident Prevention Bureau to work with local media outlets in an effort to curb traffic accidents. Most significantly, he formed the Cleveland Police Emergency Mobile Patrol, the first forerunner of the modern paramedic and EMT programs.

In addition to fighting organized crime, police officers across the country had to fight the "Public Enemy" outlaws during the 1930s, like John Dillinger, Pretty Boy Floyd, Baby Face Nelson, and Bonnie and Clyde. In an attempt to better coordinate their chases and manhunts, police departments started using two way radios by the middle of the decade. Ness made sure that two way radios were installed in all police cars, and he also authorized the purchase of 32 new squad cars and 30 new motorcycles. Ness even created a system where citizens could call one number to report any kind of emergency, similar to the modern 911 system. These programs had a major impact on Cleveland and became prototypes for much of the rest of the country.

By the end of 1939, Ness was beginning to feel like he'd accomplished everything he came to Cleveland to do. By this time he had married Evaline McAndrew and was ready for a change of location. According to author Steven Nickel:

"The final two years that Eliot Ness served as safety director were relatively quiet and, for some, disappointing. Ness was by no means idle, but it was obvious that he no longer possessed the zest and urgency with which he had formerly approached his work. It was also apparent that since marrying Evaline, Ness was spending less time on the job; the couple had become part of Cleveland society, hobnobbing with the wealthy, attending numerous social engagements, and entertaining frequently and lavishly at their new Lakewood boat house." (Torso: The Story of Eliot Ness and the Search for a Psychopathic Killer (Oct 1, 2001)

For the rest of his career, the former golden boy would make one bad decision after another. First, he took a part-time job as a consultant on the Federal Social Protection Program, an anti-venereal disease taskforce. This forced him to spend more and more time away from Cleveland and in Washington, D.C. In addition to taking him away from his new wife, it also took him away from the work he was expected to focus on in Cleveland.

In spite of his lackluster performance, Mayor Bruton's successor, Frank Lausche, still kept Ness on as safety director, much to the delight of the local press:

"Mayor Lausche today reappointed Eliot Ness safety director. It is a safe guess that he will never confront a decision more difficult politically, or one in which he will be subjected to greater pressure from opposing sides. Director Ness was obviously the most valuable asset of the Burton administration in its first two terms. His work in helping to convict eight crooked union official and a like number of corrupt police officers deserves the highest praise."

In the wee hours of the morning of March 5, 1942, Ness made a terrible mistake that truly represents what his life by this time had become. Driving his wife and two other passengers after a night of partying, he lost control of his car and collided with 21 year old Robert Sims. While no one was seriously injured, the public was outraged when they heard about the accident, and especially how Ness had left after giving Sims his name. A few months later Ness resigned and went to work for the Social Protection Program full time.

Still, it would not be fair to conclude that Ness left his position in disgrace. In fact, he was lauded in several newspapers for his work cleaning up Cleveland:

"First of all, Cleveland is a different place than it was when Eliot Ness became the safety director in 1935. Most people will agree that it is a much better place now. For instance: policemen no longer have to tip their hats when they pass a gangster on the street. Labor racketeers no longer parade down Euclid Avenue in limousines bearing placards deriding the public and law enforcement in general. Motorist have been taught and tamed into killing only about half as many people as they used to slaughter.

We may never again achieve the heights of law enforcement and competence, which have been built up during his six-year administration. It is so outstanding among American city experiences as to be a little amazing...When he took office, the town was ridden with crooked police and crooked labor bosses. A dozen such were sent to prison and scores of others scared into resignation or inactivity. There were gambling halls in every block and lush casinos in the suburbs. The little joints mostly folded and finally the big joints quit when a couple of Ness' honest cops were put in the sheriff's office. The town reached such a condition of comparative purity that about all the continual critics had to complain about was occasional bingo, strip-teasers and some policy games."

Chapter 12: Unredeemable

Ness' next stop was Washington, D. C. where he and Evaline moved in to an elegant home the government furnished for them. Ness immediately threw himself into his work with the same fervor with which he had fought the mob. In addition to designing interesting educational programs to educate men to the dangers of sexually transmitted diseases, he also worked with local army bases to discourage prostitutes from working nearby.

Unfortunately, Evaline did not like the lifestyle that went along with her husband's new job. She left him in 1944 and moved back to New York. He soon filed for divorce, citing "gross neglect and extreme cruelty" as grounds. He then left government work entirely to take become chairman of the board of the Diebold Corporation in Canton, Ohio. Once there he cut off the deadwood and restructured the organization along more profitable lines. He also recommended that the company diversify from locks and safes to also producing plastics and microfilming equipment. He even brokered a merger with York Safe and Lock Company, their primary competitor.

On one of his company trips to New York, Ness met Betty Anderson Seaver, a middle aged divorcee and artist. They married in Baltimore in 1946 and the following year they adopted a son, whom they named Robert Warren Ness.

Ness was showing sharp business acumen and was considered something of a tycoon by this time. His advice and expertise allowed him to start two ventures of his own. The first was The Middle East Company, an import-export firm that he founded with two long time business friends. The other, The Far East Company, imported silk from China to sell in the United States. Unfortunately, these ventures, though successful, were short lived due to changes in the U. S. import/export laws.

Moreover, business simply did not thrill Ness like public service did. Thus, in 1947, he decided to do the one thing he'd always avoided: go into politics. He ran for mayor of Cleveland in 1947 as an independent. Ironically, had he run as a Republican back in 1941 when he was at the height of his popularity, he probably would have won. Even so, the Republican Party still supported him against the incumbent, Democrat Thomas Burke, because they felt he was a better candidate than anyone they had in their party.

An old billboard advertisement for Ness

Not surprisingly, Ness ran on a law and order ticket, promising to cut down on purse snatchings and muggings while strengthening police presence in the community. Unfortunately, while Ness had the support of local businessmen, he was considered by the blue collar workers of the city to be anti-labor because of his hard-nosed response to the strikes of 1937. When he lost the election by a landslide, he also lost his savings and much of his will to go on.

Following the election, Ness found that the only place where he still felt at home was in the bars he frequented. There men would buy him drinks and thank him for all he'd done to make them safer, while naturally asking for one story after another of his exploits. Fortunately, only those nearest him were aware that Ness's account of those stories grew with time.

Deeply in debt, Ness spent the rest of his life working anywhere that would hire him, often being let go after only a few months because his drinking made him so unreliable. Things began to look a little better when he was hired by the Guaranty Paper Corporation in 1953. He moved with his family from Cleveland to a small town in Pennsylvania where the watermarking company could operate with a lower overhead and rented a small, comfortable house. It was there that he died suddenly of a massive heart attack on May 16, 1957. He was 54 years old.

Perhaps the most valuable thing Ness left the world, besides law and order, was a 21 page manuscript about his time chasing Capone. In addition to that more low-key and accurate account, Ness had spent the last years of his life working with writer Oscar Fraley on an account of his time tracking Capone. That book, which would become *The Untouchables*, would be published a month after his death.

The book was clearly and intentionally sensationalized in an effort to appeal to readers, and the book created a string of fictional characters and events to add suspense to the story. Though it did not translate into strong sales for the book, Ness would be immortalized by television and movie spin-offs centered around it. Over half a century after he helped end Scarface's reign in Chicago, Eliot Ness was a household name across America, and he came to be defined as the "Untouchable" hero who was both tough as nails and completely clean. In essence, the Ness portrayed by Robert Stack and Kevin Costner was the perfect cop and perfect detective rolled into one.

While the Oscar-winning film and television series might not have accurately depicted Ness as he truly was, his life and work certainly were worth celebrating.

Chapter 13: Capone the Man and Capone the Myth

Despite his fame and high profile, Al Capone was hardly a model citizen, and there's no case to be made that he was on any level a good man. He was directly and indirectly responsible for the deaths of dozens of men. Perhaps, given the distorting effects of late-stage syphilis on his personality, it's impossible to know for certain who the "real" Capone was, but he was nonetheless a complicated man with surprising and unexpected dimensions.

A number of reporters and law enforcement officials, even those who disapproved of him and his lifestyle, found him charming and gracious. Those who spent time with him during his Lansing retreat, in particular, remember him as quite the opposite of the ruthless gangster portrayed in the media. In a period of American history characterized by narrow ethnic loyalty, Capone displayed a remarkable openness. He married an Irish girl. Among his associates and close friends were not only fellow Italians, but Irish and Jews. Finally, in addition to a love of opera (to be expected of someone of Italian heritage), Capone had a real love for the true music of the age: jazz. Not only did he love the music, he expressed a genuine affection for the men who played it—black musicians, at a time when the best blacks could expect was a kind of benign hostility. In contrast to his brother Ralph, for example (the actual manager of the Capone-run Cotton Club in Cicero), Al made a point of reaching out to and sometimes assisting the musicians who passed through.

With his dramatic life and outsized personality, it was perhaps inevitable that Capone the man would be swallowed up by Capone the myth. But two developments of the 1930s even further hastened the mythologizing of Al Capone. The first was a string of movies and books playing on (and often glamorizing) gangsters in the Capone mold. Notable among these were *Little Caesar*, starring Edwin G. Robinson, and the Howard Hawks-directed *Scarface* (later remade into a story about a Cuban gangster starring Al Pacino). It is also no accident that the comic strip *Dick Tracy* (often featuring larger-than-life gangsters bearing Tommy guns) debuted around this time. And, in real life, the Depression-era 30s ushered in a new breed of outlaw: including "Baby Face" Nelson, "Pretty Boy" Floyd, Bonnie and Clyde—and, most famously, John Dillinger, who topped the FBI's Most Wanted list just as Capone had topped the earlier Public Enemies list. Whereas Capone was the ultimate insider, and fundamentally a capitalist and businessman, the new breed consisted of outsiders and renegades, reflecting the alienation and disaffection of the era. Yet somehow in the public imagination, and in their many representations since in movies especially, the outlaws of the 20s and 30s have become fused and muddled.

To this day, the image of Capone continues to be evoked in the popular culture. Behind the curtain, the man himself remains a mystery.

Bibliography

Badal, James Jessen. *In the Wake of the Butcher: Cleveland's Torso Murders*. The Kent State University Press, 2001

Bayer, Oliver Weld, editors. *Cleveland Murders*. New York: Duell, Sloan & Pearce, 1947.

Bergreen, Laurence. *Capone: The Man and the Era*. New York: Touchstone, 1994.

Condon, George E. *Cleveland: The Best Kept Secret*. New York: Doubleday & Company, 1967.

Fraley, Oscar. *Four against the Mob*. New York: Award Books, 1976.

Fraley, Oscar and Paul Robsky. *The Last of the Untouchables*. New York: Pocket Books, 1988

Heimel, Paul W., *Eliot Ness: The Real Story*. Coudersport, PA: Knox Books, 1997.

Kobler, John. *The Life and World of Al Capone*. New York: G.P. Putnam's Sons,1971.

Martin, John Bartlow. *Butcher's Dozen and Other Murders*. New York: Harper & Brothers, 1950.

Meyers, Richard. *TV Detectives*. San Diego, CA: A.S. Barnes & Co., 1981.

Ness, Eliot, and Oscar Fraley. *Untouchables*. Englewood Cliffs, NJ: Julian Messner, 1957.

Nickel, Steven, Torso: *The True Story of Eliot Ness & the Search for a Psychopathic Killer*. Winston-Salem, NC: John F. Blair, 1989.

Porter, Philip W. *Cleveland: Confused City on a Seesaw*. Columbus, OH: Ohio State University Press, 1976.

Rasmussen, William T. *Corroborating Evidence*. Sunstone Press, 2006

Schoenberg, Robert J. *Mr. Capone: The Real -and Complete-Story of Al Capone*. New York: William Morrow & Company, 1992.

CPSIA information can be obtained
at www.ICGtesting.com
Printed in the USA
LVHW080214300321
682931LV00014B/387